Whe_ Grow Up

By Marcie Aboff

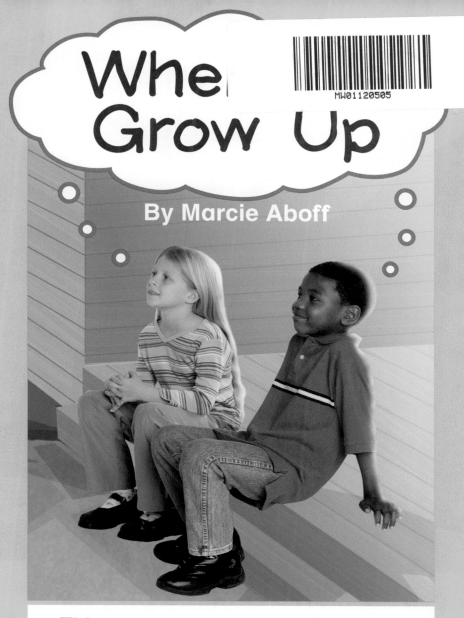

This story is about two children who think about what they will be when they grow up. As you read, think about what you would like to be when you grow up.

PEARSON

■ Anna and Matt watched the sun setting over the mountains. As they watched the sunset, they heard the roar of an airplane. They looked up and saw a plane high above them. Matt watched the plane **soar** over the mountains.

"When I grow up, maybe I'll be an airplane pilot," Matt said. "I would **soar** high into the sky. I would fly over mountains. I would fly to many new places."

3

 "That would be fun," said Anna. "But I'd like to be a captain on a big ship when I grow up. I would sail across the ocean. I would look out for whales and dolphins and other ships at sea."

"I could go with you on your ship," Matt said. "I'd be a diver. I would dive deep into the sea. I'd find plants and animals that live in the ocean. I'd make friends with dolphins and whales."

"That's a good plan," Anna said. "But maybe I'll be an animal trainer in a circus. I'd wear a fancy **costume**. I'd be kind to the animals so they would have fun learning new tricks. The dogs would dance on their hind legs and jump through hoops. The elephants would hold each other's tail and walk in a big circle."

"Maybe I'll be a clown," said Matt. "I would wear a funny **costume**. I would give balloons to all the children. I would do many tricks. I'd juggle three balls at once."

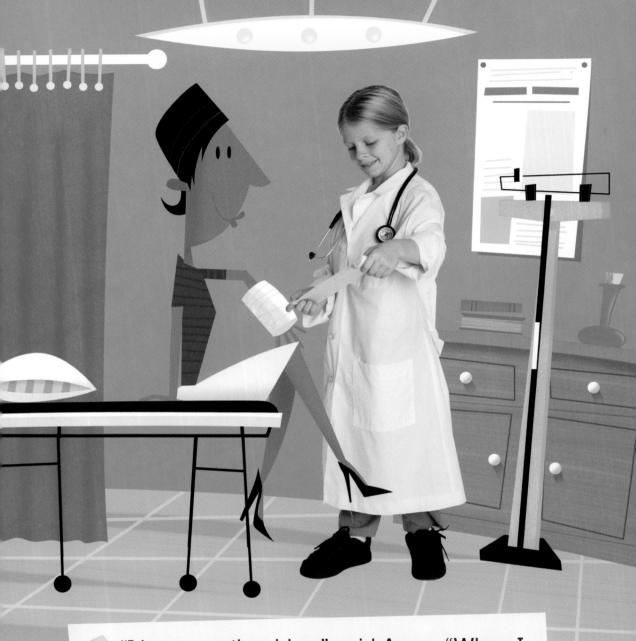

"I have another idea," said Anna. "When I grow up, I might be a doctor. I would wear a long, white coat. When people get sick, I'd make them feel better. I'd fix their broken bones. I'd help people get healthy again."

🔵 "Maybe I'll be a doctor for children," said Matt. "I would wear a long, white coat, too. I would take care of babies. I would help children grow up to be healthy and strong."

9

"Maybe I'll be a teacher," said Anna. "I would help children learn new things. I would teach them their ABC's and how to count to 100. I would help them learn to read."

10

"Maybe I'll work in a library," said Matt. "I would help people find books to read. My library would have funny books and books about animals. There would be sports books, too."

"Maybe I'll be a soccer player," Anna said. "I would **dribble** the ball down the field. Then I'd pass the ball to one of my teammates. She would pass the ball back to me. Then I'd kick the ball right into the net. Goal! The crowd would cheer for me."

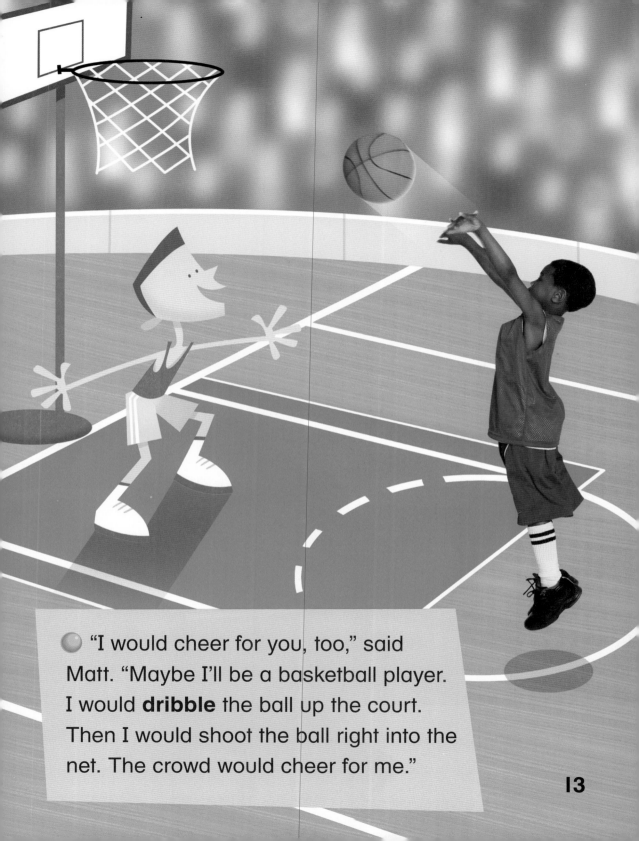

"I would cheer for you, too," said Matt. "Maybe I'll be a basketball player. I would **dribble** the ball up the court. Then I would shoot the ball right into the net. The crowd would cheer for me."

13

 Anna and Matt sat quietly for a while. Stars began to shine across the dark night sky. Anna looked up at the stars. She said, "Maybe I'll be an **astronaut** and fly to the Moon."

 Matt looked up at the Moon. "I can be an **astronaut**, too. I can be an airplane pilot, a diver, or a doctor. I can be a clown or a basketball player. I can be anything I want to be when I grow up. So can you!"

Glossary

astronaut someone who is trained to travel into space on a spacecraft

costume clothing that helps a person pretend to be someone or something else

dribble to move a ball with many light bounces or kicks

soar to rise or move up